Also by Zoë Brigley

POETRY:

The Secret, (Bloodaxe, 2007)

Conquest, (Bloodaxe, 2012)

Hand & Skull, (Bloodaxe, 2019)

Aubade After a French Movie, (Broken Sleep, 2020).

100 Poems to Save the Earth [editor], (Seren, 2021)

ESSAYS:

Notes from a Swing State, (Parthian, 2019)

Also by Kristian Evans

Unleaving, (Happenstance, 2015)

100 Poems to Save the Earth [editor], (Seren, 2021)

OTHERWORLDS:

ESSAYS & LETTERS ON NATURE & MAGIC

Brigley, Evans

ISBN: 978-1-913642-62-4

Cover design by Aaron Kent

Edited & typeset by Aaron Kent

Broken Sleep Books (2021)

Broken Sleep Books Ltd
Rhydwen,
Talgarreg,
SA44 4HB
Wales

Contents

For Gwion, Oscar, Ted & James

Otherworlds

Zoë Brigley & Kristian Evans

Otherworlds

Zoë Brigley

c/w miscarriage

IN the winter before the COVID-19 pandemic takes hold in the U.S., my children and I take a trip to an abandoned shopping mall. Run-down malls have a symbolic significance in America: a legacy of the 2000s and the terrible recession that many places have never really shaken. In *Gone Girl,* Gillian Flynn, describes a bankrupt mall in mythical terms as "two million square feet of echo." In the novel, the empty mall is left to criminals and the poor, but here I am driving under the cracked mall signage, entering a nondescript and beat-up storefront with my two small kids.

We come to see a phenomenon called Otherworld, a "32,000 square foot immersive art installation" in Columbus. The blurb on the website promises "Mysteries unfold as you explore over 40 rooms filled with large-scale interactive art, mixed reality playgrounds and secret passageways. It's an all new kind of art experience where visitors are encouraged to freely explore and interact with a surreal world of science fiction and fantasy."

The day I visit with my kids, I have a hard time getting the eldest inside. The entrance is a David Lynch style corridor hung with red velvet curtains. But once in, the children soon get into the spirit of things. They climb into a huge red mouth, burrow into the belly of a hairy monster, and find inside it a beating heart. There is a room with mirrors where we are refracted and reflected a hundred times, a room where opening a coffin turns the light from sepia to technicolor, a room like a mad scientist's laboratory. We fly through the corridors, the twists and turns, test the limits of the 32,000 feet.

But while the children play, something bothers me. In one room, a plastic tree unfurls at the center. In another, stars glimmer on the ceiling, while in another fish are projected on the walls. These are the rooms I like the least. What are we seeking in these human-made replicas?

The children seem dissatisfied now. "Is that all there is?" asks the youngest, as we take a turn through the rooms for the third time. Whatever pleasures there are in lights, colour, and mirrors, there is something superficial about it all, and I can't help thinking of the site's former use: probably a department store in its prime, jewel of American consumerism and high capitalism. But what is it that we are being sold here with all this spectacle?

When my ex-husband picks us up in the litter-strewn lot of the empty mall, he asks me how it went, and tell him that it was amazing, magical, fun. What I don't mention is a nagging feeling. What I don't say is that something about Otherworld is ultimately unsatisfying.

Fast forward to spring, and we are in lockdown in Ohio. I read the news anxiously about potential social distancing and my family in the UK. I lie awake at night thinking about older relatives at risk back in Wales. I am relieved when the lockdown comes to the UK too. In the US and UK we are forced to stay in our homes, only leaving for trips to the supermarket or daily exercise in the local area.

But when the lockdown comes, when social worlds are closed to us, something strange happens. The British newspapers print photographs of queues of cars in the Snowdonia National Park, and U.K. beaches are bustling despite the lockdown. The first weekend of the lockdown here in Ohio, we drive to a local lake that is normally a quiet spot, but we turn back from the main carpark because the lot is overflowing with cars. Further down the lakeshore, we find a quiet place to park. At the lakeside, a group of people gather, despite the warnings, to be baptized. A white man in a baseball cap lowers them one by one into the murky water, shouting: "In the name of the father and the son and the holy ghost." Through his binoculars, our eldest kid watches crowds of people walking across the dam to see the views.

What is this logic? How strange that the first instinct of many is to visit spectacular sites of nature or holiday spots despite the warnings about social distancing. I remember the visitors to Otherworld, charging around the dark interior, demanding to be entertained, circling around the same rooms over and over again. Are we making nature our immersive experience now that places like Otherworld are off-limits?

Now the circle closes. To flatten the curve, we stay in our local area, on our daily exercise forced to examine unspectacular paths and everyday hedges. But is there something we could find there, something more nourishing and less superficial?

The ancient Celts believed in an Otherworld. In Welsh and Irish myth, the Otherworld existed beside our own, on the edge of where we were living, and on occasion intruding or inviting visitors in. The hero would find a ball of silver thread rolling away into a mist that would be a portal to a world that was not our own but filled with the things that we like to forget or ignore.

In the shutdown, I am caught in the circle of my own neighborhood, but it is not for the first time. This time last year, I was grieving a late and terrible miscarriage. I saw no one, went no further than my house if I could help it, but I found myself walking the railroad tracks a few streets away from my house. I would wander through the woods, and at first, I found nothing remarkable. That spring, branches moved faintly in the wind, and the white and purple hepatica flowers pushed daintily through leaf litter under the trees.

But maybe the ball of twine left for us follow is the edge of a real Otherworld, because we have seldom as a culture appreciated the eeriness and beauty of nature in its most mundane and unspectacular forms. When I was grieving and walking in the scrubby woods last year, I felt a sudden relief when a thought struck me that even here, everything was animated and lit with eerie beauty.

There is nothing good about COVID-19, nothing that can make up for the deaths, the illness, the institutional blunders and mis-steps, the losses, but if we must endure it, perhaps there is something we can admit. As we try to survive physically and mentally in lockdown, we are being forced to pay attention. We are being asked to look at how we are living. We are stepping out of the spectacle of capitalism, and although we treat the earth and nature with routine contempt, the world does not revolve around human beings. It never did. There is an Otherworld beyond humans, and it is awake. It has always been awake.

A Letter About Dwelling

From Kristian to Zoë

TO begin a conversation about dwelling and environmental ethics, I have to be honest – and it's a bit scandalous of me to say it – I don't really like talking about climate change. It's too abstract, too judgemental, too impossible. It almost forces us into a posture of mourning and guilt… as this big abstract monster looms over us. I think about mass extinction rather than climate these days, as it has a more immediate reality. And it's sobering to remember that humans too are on the list of at-risk species.

But I definitely see our approach to ecologies as beginning in human relationships. In the domestic, certainly. In the hearth-light, and at its smudged and shifting boundary. Our response to the disasters of mass extinction must begin at "home" in the person too – we can't immediately stop using plastic or fossil fuel, but we can try to see and hear more carefully, with more alertness… more ecologically. And really, if we can shift our perspective in that way, it can lead us into some very strange and interesting thoughts, and we might begin to see a future in which we really want to live...

Does seeing the 'Person' in the 'Other,' and thus implicitly recognising a self-hood, rather than something alien or offensive or repulsive, require a particular quality of attention? Gentleness, care, openness, listening? It seems so easy these days to dehumanise – perhaps because so much of our interaction and conduct is mediated by the Internet – and often we fail to really notice the world and each other until it's too late. We are causing a mass extinction, but when we struggle to even see each other as persons, our neighbours, lovers, guests, how can we even begin to see the vast losses the world is suffering?

Maybe we should turn to the very attentive way in which young kids listen to the voices of the world, and how they understand the "selving" of the world (to borrow from G.M. Hopkins) in the way they relate in play and how they instinctively include other species as persons.

We can say that for the last few hundred years Western culture has privileged the eye, and the perspective, and the seeing of things as trajectories from a to b: the march of progress, evolution, the infinite distance... but maybe now we are shifting to the ear, to listening to the whole surroundings (the environs, the circum-stances), tilting an ear in the direction of travel, to meandering and turning and returning, and listening again: the perpetual renewal of the eternal present. Maybe our "listening" is the best gift we have to offer each other right now. Is poetry showing a shift to music recently, to hearing? I wonder.

Mugwort

Kristian Evans

> *The invisible of the invisible is the visible. The other side
> of the other side is this side. If the body hides the soul, then
> the soul hides the body as well: the "soul" of the soul is the
> body and the "body" of the body is the soul.*
> —Eduardo Viveiros de Castro

I don't know how she got here or where she came from, but there she is, seven feet tall and standing in the potato patch, and now I can't imagine the garden without her. How often have I drifted away from work lately to stand lulled in her shade? Bindweed is climbing the onions, there are butterflies cavorting among the broccoli, I should probably renew contact with my neighbours – but look at her. Idly I stroke the silvery down of her leaves, soft as mouse fur. I rub her flower buds between my palms, breathe their forthright aroma. I daydream of ancient villages in endless forests, the other-side of the hedge: dancers with the eyes of bees, courteous wolves, alien traders with dubious goods, lengthening shadows and an unexpected fork in the road.

That otherwise reliable guide, *Flora Brittanica*, says she can grow up to four feet tall. My mugwort is surely going to double that. Weeds? No such thing. Lately I've been returning to forgotten ideas, studying clairvoyants and visionaries like Jacob Boehme and Rudolf Steiner, magicians and makers of potions, like Paracelsus: *"As a tree or a plant grows out of its seed, so the new life grows out of the old one, and that which was heretofore invisible becomes visible."*

But mugwort has always inspired superstitions, and strange ideas. Of course, I try to keep my mind open, but not so open that absolutely anything can get in. Here in Wales it was the custom to hang sprays of mugwort over the entrances to houses on St. John's Eve to protect the dwellers from evil. Throughout Europe, the plant is associated with midsummer – the strength of the sun – and the banishing of dark spirits. There's a curious almost world-wide consensus that mugwort protects the traveller from tiredness, wild animals, and sunstroke. An old Scottish story records the words of a mermaid, a selkie, a seal-woman, who observing the funeral of a girl who died of consumption, sang out this verse as she swam through the bay:

> If they wad drink nettles in March,
> And eat muggons (mugwort) in May,
> Sae mony braw maidens
> Wadna gang to the clay.

Artemisia vulgaris. The name comes from the virginal Greek goddess of the wild and of childbirth. In the ancient story, Actaeon, a young hunter, glimpses the naked Artemis as she is bathing in a lake. There are different versions of what happened next, but most agree that Actaeon was punished by being transformed into a stag – while retaining his human mind – and was hunted to exhaustion by his own hounds, torn to pieces.

Modern day witches suggest that smoking mugwort can alter the perceptions and induce lucid dreaming. I give it a try. I pick some leaves and dry them on a plate in the noon heat. Later, as the sun is going down, I crumble them into my pipe and take a few tentative puffs. The taste is quite pleasant, bitter sage and old moss, wild thyme; but nothing much happens. Everything carries on as normal. It's unlikely that mugwort will be outlawed any time soon. But who knows how these things work? Because that night I do indeed have a vivid dream…

I'm standing in my kitchen, struggling to open a giant fridge. I'm not strong enough, but I tug and heave and finally it bursts open and huge bales and bushels of mugwort leaf pour out and unfold themselves, covering the floor – and now the door is open I can't shut it and the leaves continue to pour out. I open a cupboard and the same thing happens: a torrent of mugwort filling the kitchen up to my waist so that I'm wading in leaves and some of them are popping like gorse pods and turning into mice - mugwort popcorn - and the mice are scampering everywhere and everything I touch turns into mugwort and pops and turns into mice and I'm drowning and I begin to panic and then I notice her. Sitting calmly at the kitchen table. A seven foot tall woman with skin the colour of a sand lizard and a smile as inscrutable as the Artemis of Ephesus. I tried to speak. What did I want to say: *Yes*? Or perhaps it was *No*? But my tongue was a mugwort leaf and my lungs were full of pollen as fine as the dust on a moth's wings.

When I woke I still felt the shock of the fright, the chill running down my spine. But later, recording the dream, distance restored, I smirk at myself. I'll keep this one private, that's for sure. The biologist JBS Haldane suggested that "the universe is not only queerer than we suppose, it is queerer than we can suppose." So maybe we are wrong to think that only humans can be persons. Maybe consciousness exists beyond humans and matter is not dead and inert. Maybe it's actually just sleeping and dreaming. And maybe in dreams, it can communicate.

I check no one is watching and then I strike a match, light a stick of incense. A ribbon of sweet myrrh mutters to itself as I poke the stick into the earth under the mugwort bush. Pascale's wager perhaps, but suddenly I pray that if the dreamer awakes, it will not be vengeful, it will not seek justice, and that maybe, somehow, it will be able to forgive us.

I listen for a moment, unsure, unsteady, dizzy almost. And then I light another stick, certain that one is nowhere near enough.

A Letter About the Emptying Field

From Zoë to Kristian

I'M so happy that you recognize what I was saying about dwelling extending in and through nature into our social relationships. I loved the adjectives you used: gentleness, care, openness, listening. In fact, what you said about listening could be key. On the other side though is the refusal to listen. Is dehumanising similar to seeing nature as merely there to provide sustenance?

Meanwhile, I am back in the U.S., and it's not an easy time. Over the weekend you probably saw there were two mass shootings – one in Texas and another just down the road in Dayton, Ohio. So many here live in the shadow of potential violence all the time.

Also, many Midwesterners don't pay much attention to climate change because they are preoccupied with being at war with nature, which has a much more hostile aspect than it does in Britain. They are always trying to manicure gardens, fields, and parks; battling poison ivy, poison sumac, and poison oak, ticks, mosquitoes, carpenter ants, brown recluse spiders with their necrotic bite, termites, floods, tornadoes, polar vortex cold, extreme heat in the summer, golf-ball-sized hailstones or high winds, possums, raccoons, coyotes, and even the occasional bear or wolf. I don't think that these things are unrelated: the routine violence, conformity in the Midwest, and the battle with nature.

I live in a town on the outskirts of the city, as close to nature as I can be, and here I am graced with beautiful visitors. Red cardinals in the snow, or now in summer, deer come to eat the blueberries from my garden, and just yesterday there were hummingbirds in the garden probing their long beaks into the flowers. Water snakes sidle their way along the creek. The wild geese flying high and sharp in formation. All that is my favourite part of being in America and I am planning some trips to keep the wilderness inside alive.

I'm re-reading what you said here: "often we fail to really notice the world and each other until it's too late"; and it puts me in mind of one of my favourite poems by Rachel McKibbens: 'Into the Dark and Emptying Field' from the collection of the same name. After an argument with her lover, a woman invites him to look through a brass keyhole into her skull. Inside he sees something incredible: a field of glorious horses, free to run on their elegant legs, but what the man sees is not enough for him. The interaction becomes dominating, coercive. The man demands more, but all he is left with is the 'dark and emptying field' of the poem's title as the horses gallop away. I always find that last line devastating in its new context in the light of the loss for the woman.

Daphne Becoming

Zoë Brigley

c/w violence against women

SO imagine this: I am sixteen or seventeen years old, and I have been seeing an older man for over a year, a man who is often sexually abusive and coercive. I am walking away one evening from the house where he lives on a suburban street, and I am stiff and sore. I know I am trapped, because though I want to leave him, he has made me feel that he is the only man, the only person who will ever love me. I still hope that if I can make him love me enough, one day he might stop.

When I am being hurt, I think of myself as becoming wood, becoming a tree. I'm not the first woman to feel this way. This was confirmed for me when I read Alice Walker's defiant novel *The Color Purple* where the women there too described their reaction on suffering pain as turning to wood.

It is no coincidence either that all those women pursued in Ovid turn into trees, reeds, or plants. In the myths, it is a kind of escape. Chased by Apollo, Daphne finds herself trapped, and her transformation is tinged with horror. 'Her feet benumb'd and fastened to the ground,' she grows a 'filmy' and protective rind, as her arms turn to branches. Ovid is not a totally sympathetic narrator; he tells us salaciously that Daphne cannot hide 'the smoothness of her skin,' and describes Apollo kissing it. She is only half-transformed. Becoming wood is a frail defense for a person being harmed. Becoming the tree is not a true escape then, because even while the transformation to a laurel makes Daphne strange and non-human, she is still vulnerable to attack.

But let's get back to me at 16. I pass through an alley and come out onto a wide green lawn. I stop under a tree, and across the grass is the shape of turrets, the castle that crowns the naval of the town where I grew up. I am standing under an oak tree, pulling my denim jacket closed around me, because a breeze has started blowing from the west. The canopy of the oak is alive with leaves blinking and trembling.

Would you believe me if I told you that every tree sings a particular song when the wind blows through it? That day the oak is singing but not to me especially. We enjoy humanizing nature, framing it as a friend or family. Maybe it began in the nineteenth century with Darwin who described the behaviors of animals and insects in peculiarly human terms. Writing for *The Guardian* about how nature healed her alcohol addiction, Lucy Jones uses a maternal image of nursing: "I rested in her care for a while." But nature is not our mother, is not human even, and it is not there simply to be used by us as some kind of alternative therapy or rehab. "Nature" does not even exist as a separate entity from human beings. And, no, the oak tree that day is not singing for me, or to me. Despite that, I am moved by it, and the wind moves sensuously through my hair, over my lips and cheeks, just as it moves the slender branches and murmuring leaves.

I am suffering that day. I am physically hurting, and I am broken by the repetition of what happens when this man gets me alone, when I make myself quiet and small and faraway. What happens in the house makes me alert, watchful, skittish perhaps, my body tense with what occurs over and over again.

Trees are vulnerable too, and they are treated with same carelessness as women. Both are seen as disposable. Here in Ohio, I live on the outskirts of Columbus, a city where the building and expansion is busting out into the countryside. One day, I am driving the kids out to a lake through a suburb that was once a lonely road with just one tackle and bait store. Turning a corner, we come upon a devastating scene. Row upon row of ancient trees have been cut down, their stumps poke up, trunks left where they fell, abandoned. The fallen wood looks black under a grey sky, and in the midst, a nicely painted red barn sits unexpected, comic: a barn once shaded by the foliage now stripped. I wonder, how could someone look at this and not be moved?

But perhaps lack of empathy is precisely the problem, not

only for nature but for women. Because some human beings, especially privileged ones, have a hard time projecting themselves into the world around them. Or worse still, with the sociopaths in our midst, there is a terrible kind of empathy where an aggressor enjoys inflicting damage, delights precisely in understanding the harm they are doing to people, or to creatures, or even gets off on it.

Perhaps what is most precious is not only the ability to empathize, but the ability to actively take joy in what is alive around us. This might be what heals us: when we can feel a sense of our own unimportance in relation to other people and creatures and things.

Like that day when I stand under the oak tree as a teenager, feeling my wounds sharply. But something about the tree changes that, because the oak is alive. The wind sings through it. The leaves are alive, the trunk is alive, the roots are alive, and the earth is alive, and so, even I am alive and feeling the shuddering world. Somehow this moment makes me stronger, and of course eventually I leave that man.

Trees persist despite the carelessness of humans, despite the assumption that nothing is as important as our appetites, and that nature must bend to our will. All of a sudden though, people are waking up and realizing that the absence of trees, the sterilization of nature around them is making them sick. Lucy Jones, again, writes with surprise that her alcohol addiction was cured by walks at a local marsh in London. Her argument is that we need to maintain and keep the natural world alive because human beings need it, but isn't this just another dead end?

Because though the oak tree that I stood under offered healing in that moment, that restoration was not its reason for being. It is abusive to think about creatures and things that way, mirroring the abuser of women, who sees their lover as solely existing as a lever for their own desires and wants, without any needs of their own. It is not uncommon though, so in the nasty, little book (supposedly for children), *The Giving Tree*, Shel Silverstein directly overlaps the woman and tree as objects that must simply give up everything they have until nothing remains. But where does that leave us?

Because if creatures and natural objects can heal us, it is not in a sanitized, manicured version of "Nature". When the oak tree strikes me with its power, it is not because I see it as an all-sacrificing mother, not some kind of egotistical idea that the tree is there for me to heal me. When I experience healing, it is because of the tree's strangeness, because of how eerie and nonhuman it seems as the wind blows through it. It is healing because I realize how little I know of it, and the tree gives me this just by being alive.

Is this an answer to trauma? The living ecologies around us? And if they do heal us, is it not because they resemble human care but precisely because they couldn't care less about us? Couldn't it be that we are removed from trauma by what is strange and eerie about nature? By how removed it is from constraints, from sanitized human environments, from the perverse dysfunctions of the human world where men abuse and kill women with sad regularity?

I have gone back to this moment again and again: just a sixteen-year-old girl standing under an oaks tree, clutching her jacket around her. It wouldn't look like much to an observer, and I have struggled to understand its significance myself. But I know how important it is as one of a series of moments that led me at last to break away from my abuser, led me to the day when I set myself free.

And now we find ourselves in a moment on the edge of catastrophe, because white Western politicians mirror my abuser. Either they fail to empathize with people, creatures, and things, or they actually take pleasure in destroying them. It is up to us to feel the shuddering world, to protect it, because the trees are caught in their roots and bark, caught like Daphne in her laurel form, caught by the whims of privileged men. But could we change that? Could we set Daphne free? And in doing so, could we free ourselves?

A Letter About Homelessness

From Kristian to Zoë

IT sounds amazing where you live: truly wild. Britain (and I mean the geographic entity, part of a rainy Atlantic archipelago) seems so deeply and intensively negotiated with that it has a sort of... human feeling to it right down through the layers. As if the human-nature treaties have all been written up and signed-off a long time ago. As if there are so many human ghosts in the soil now, that there is a noticeably human face and fragrance to all things. So many human ghosts.

I encountered lots of 'eerie' things here growing up on the edge of the dunes, wandering off alone – running away. But the dunes are not really fully present, not fully real; in a way, they are slippery, elusive, you can dissolve in them and lose track, things can get strange, a sense of incursions: odd silences occur on hot afternoons and suddenly something else is present and the hair stands up on your neck, or you might feel like you had fallen asleep for a moment, and suddenly time has flown, or you encounter an odd abandoned structure jutting from the sand. Fairy tale events. But it's never quite completely out of control, it never feels wild or deadly like a mountain lion... it always has at least a partly human signature.

But the US, however, is so huge – well, it seems to me as if the ghosts out there are all wild, and not very human at all. The American eerie, I imagine, is genuinely dangerous, and heedless of the human. Those vast mind-boggling wildernesses. It's interesting that Britain would almost completely disappear if you dropped it into the United States, like a rock into the sea.

We've got such a big a problem here in Britain, because our self-image just does not match up at all to the reality now. We think we are a superpower, but we really aren't. And I guess when self-image and self don't match up... when they contradict each other, as they do in Britain... well I suppose that's a recipe for madness. There's a sense of slippage, a dissociation in the national psyche.

I can't imagine what it must be like to suffer those constant gun attacks over there though...it's just bizarre, completely appalling. A virus, an infection that keeps flaring up. I love the idea of America's wild beauty, the native stories and languages – but the culture there today seems terrifying and authoritarian – the white supremacy, the police killings, the border camps etc.

Your mention of our need to expand ideas of manhood reminded me of a troubling article on body dysmorphia in men in *The Guardian* which makes the point that in the 70s men were supposed to look like David Bowie, but now, they are supposed to look like Navy Seals or whatever. That we are seeing a rise of intolerance and fascist ideas with the growth of the alt-right etc is surely not unrelated.

It's worth remembering that the Green movement historically has been driven by the white middle and upper classes; it has attracted racists and eugenicists. Henry Williamson, author of *Tarka the Otter* was a supporter of Mosely and Hitler. Recently, the El Paso murderer attempted to justify his actions by gesturing towards ecological concerns. It's the sort of behaviour that grows out of the old adversarial mode and mentality that got us into this mess in the first place. The fear of our fundamental homelessness as creatures of language, existing at a distance from the world. Which is our gift, really.

The Rachel McKibbens poem is devastating, shocking and true. Those horses! Reminds me superficially of the impulse behind Auden's "let the more loving one be me" but of course, Auden wasn't at risk of violence in his thoughtful loving, his body wasn't haunted by the cultural violence that stalks through the McKibbens poem.

I suppose that leads me to the opposite of dwelling. Would it be... owning? Controlling? Dominating? Maybe the dweller sits and listens or meanders and plays. So the opposite of that would be to crash through, disregard, shout, slash and burn. And an inability to value the unquantifiable. "But what is it worth?! Prove it! Demonstrate it to me in ways I can profit from!"

And that attitude returns us to ...a man alone "in the dark and emptying field."

But I hope these ideas of dwelling are like medicinal weeds and wildflowers, thriving where the ploughs and herbicides haven't reached, under the hedges, at the roadsides, remedies ready to be remembered. Not that we have much choice now...

Lapwings and Tiger Moths

Kristian Evans

HERE in the duneland, no rain for a month. Every day now, soon after dawn, the sun's heat hurries to a pitiless blaze and the sand burns the air to golden dust. Dragonflies thrive. They materialise beside us like digital updates from paradise, alerting us, alerting us – then gone.

In the dune-slack, an impassable marsh in winter, now dry and clinker brittle, the water-mint, toughened by thirst, crunches under our scuffing boots and releases its medicinal vapours; an aroma so volatile it smears itself on our scorched skins.

It clarifies the senses, sweeps the mind clean, and more importantly, conceals the taste of us from the marauding horseflies. "It's like magic," I declare, striding ahead, an excitable guide. I'd promised you magic today, after all, on our walk into the dunes, and here it is, all around us, and I am proud.

Yes, magic, the swaying grey viperweed, its hypnotic flowers of indigo and Aegean blue. Everywhere the devil's-bit and the lady's bedstraw. Hidden in the old names, a history it's tempting to trust. Fireweed and knapweed, loosestrife and toadflax. The ragwort's audacious glow is loaded with busy cinnabar moths, soldier beetles, mining bees.

We're in the otherworld now, because look, here's a dune orchid, lilac-tongued like the moon. A dragonfly appears again, and we're face to face with a hovering alphabet, a living hieroglyph.

And this is the spot where fifty years ago a boy found an old flintlock pistol, carefully concealed, treasure, perfectly preserved. He took it to school to show it off, and the headmaster confiscated it and that was that. Can you believe it?

And here come the lapwings, a bandit squadron in broken formation swooping towards us, uttering their weird challenge, engaging the intruders. Their cries an Atari soundtrack played on the uillean pipes. It's a display intended to distract us and unsettle us and keep us moving. Gorgeous birds who laughed at Christ's crucifixion.

In the old English spell books that I like to read, you will often come across 'experiments' that require a lapwing. To fetch one of the rebel angels out of the fabric of the fallen world, you must first kill a lapwing, we're told. Then you must make an ink of its blood and write the angel's name on the skin of an unborn hound.

It's said that a female lapwing will feign injury to draw egg-hunters away from her nest, offering herself as a seemingly easy meal. Perhaps it's this deceitful behaviour that first recommended her blood to magicians. It might fool foxes, but humans have plundered lapwing nests for centuries. In Victorian times the eggs were massively over-harvested, sold for nothing in London, and lapwing numbers plummeted. The once extensive flocks dwindled to straggling remnants. They've continued to decline in our own time.

It's become impossible to engage with the natural world, the bright world outside the window, without reckoning such losses, without touching the wounds and breaking every spell. We know we will find absences and fading memories. It can sometimes seem as if we're living in our own elegies.

A tiger moth alighted on my wrist last week as I read a rare transcript of "*An Excellent Booke of The Art of Magicke*" by the infamous torturer courtier Humphrey Gilbert and his scryer, John Davys, Queen Elizabeth's master navigator. The moth's extravagant beauty was astonishing even though the insect was ragged and tired. The underwing colour is as rich as Sicilian blood oranges. Its face, something dreamed up by a delirious necromancer.

Researching it later, I discovered that the tiger moth's numbers have declined by 89% in my own lifetime. They've almost disappeared. How could that have happened? In 30 years. Where have they all gone? I felt as if I had reached to stroke the softness of its fur but broken off the wings instead.

Something profound and fundamental is wrong. Are we erasing the world? Maybe that's it. Maybe we're running fast away from the best evidence of our own reality.

"Where he that knows will like a lapwing fly, farre from the nest, and so himself belie." And here is bittersweet, I say, innocent and treacherous, the country cousin of belladonna, her rambling vine weighed down with purple berries.

And here, my love, is legendary meadowsweet, smirking to herself in the mirror, applying the greasepaint, writing your name, licking the pollen from her fingertips and tasting the white soot of an owl's wings.

A Letter about Masculinity

From Zoë to Kristian

I was thinking on our conversation about men and violence today. I was surprised when you talked about south Wales being macho, but you're right: there are many damaged and hurt men in the valleys, and there is inherited violence for sure. You are right too to question the idea that the category of working class "men" only refers to white, straight men, but whatever the context, I can definitely see the predicament of having to live up to ideas of what men should be. I try to work on this with my male students by teaching texts that expand their view of conventional manhood, and who they might allow themselves to be.

I've been thinking about life after COVID-19 and the bizarre behaviors of some white men. Here in Columbus, one white man protesting lockdown was photographed carrying an anti-Semitic sign framing Jewish people as the "real virus," which was so appalling and disgusting.

Not so long ago, in our neighboring state of Michigan, armed protestors – angry about lockdown – entered government buildings to challenge Democratic Governor Gretchen Whitmer's stay-at-home order. A woman who has openly talked about experiencing sexual violence had armed and aggressive protesters calling to "lock her up," just for trying to re-open the state from lockdown with the least possible harm.

Having said all this, and still thinking about men and violence, I read an amazing poem recently by Samuel Green: 'On Patmos Kneeling in the Panagea.' It begins in the moment described by the title – kneeling in a Greek church, hearing high heels on the stone. The narrator experiences involuntary memory, which takes him back to a military hospital full of veterans suffering horrifying injuries, and the sound of nurses' heels on the hospital tiles. I understand and recognize this phenomenon – being transported by a sound or smell – which can happen as if by magic, and it can be wonderful or painful depending on where you are being transported back to. I also liked it because it describes the little acts of kindness made by the nurses for the injured men. And what if compassion and ethics of care was not just expected of women – the nurses being women in this poem – but of everyone? Small kindnesses are like acts of grace we visit on one another, and they have something to do with dwelling too.

The Laughter of Foxes

Kristian Evans

I wake to the shrieking of foxes. At first, I can't place the sound – still half-asleep, it seems like a scrap of dream has escaped into the attic or the walls, whistling and wheezing – but fully awake now, and yes, it's the foxes in the garden, back again as they have been the last few nights. I lean across the bed, gently nudge the creaking window open onto the frosty air and eavesdrop on their behaviour.

Usually, the nights are quiet here in this house among the dunes. Sometimes you can hear the sea, sometimes the distant M4 motorway. But now breeding season has begun for the foxes, and the turmoil of it echoes through the dark. The vixens are fertile for just a few nights, after midwinter. Last year's cubs are driven out to fend for themselves and they disperse clumsily through the country seeking new territory. You'll see them in the mornings in the misty lanes, looking lost.

Foxes everywhere are suddenly on the move. The older animals roam with a more certain purpose. It's when they meet that they utter their strange cries -- bark or howl or scream, it sounds eerily human, and it's always unsettling and surprising the first time you hear it. Listening at the window, my imagination conjures devils, half-formed images, shadowy faces, marginal scribbles in old bestiaries, crying and cavorting out there beyond the lamp-glow.

Foxes and devils are old companions of course. I think of Huw Llwyd, and his poem, his *cywydd*, *"Cyngor y Llwynog"*, "Fox Council". Huw was from the north, from Merioneth (hence *llwynog* instead of the southern *cadno* for fox), and his richly adventurous life has passed into legend.

A magician in the Elizabethan manner, a contemporary of John Dee and Shakespeare, Huw understood the relationship of the stars and the planets to events of earth; how everything is chained to everything else. In common with other magicians of his time, he would call and bind and interrogate the sublunar devils using techniques gleaned from banned books. He was rumoured to know how to make events shift in his favour – he was a healer, a finder, a dreamer, a man able to control his own luck. He was also, it follows, a very fine poet. *"Cyngor y Llwynog"* is an invocation of a fox spirit:

> *Good morning, fox of the cave,*
> *Every tame fowl's arch foe-man,*
> *Your ripple I recognize,*
> *Welcome to fertile country…*

The invocation has the desired effect: the fox appears. How can we prosper, he asks it, how can we achieve success in a wicked world? And the answer he receives is suitably foxy: "*Seeking success? Preferment? / I'd wish you to live… like me.*" As the poem continues however, it begins to seem that not a fox, but a devil has answered the summons, a devil in a fox-mask perhaps. The advice it offers invites indulgence in a life of wild greed, cruelty and deceit. "*Integrity today, in the world's view, is foolish.*"

The price to pay for success isn't mentioned, but it is implied. We never learn whether Huw accepted that price and struck a deal. But we do know that he is remembered as a foxhunting cunning man, a *dyn hysbys*, and that a rock in the torrent of the Cynfal river is known to this day as Huw Llwyd's pulpit, where he preached the gospel to his people by day, and by night argued and bartered with the devils of the air.

So the story goes. We no longer interrogate devils. We just hand them the reins and let them get on with it. We no longer read those banned books that fascinated old Huw Llwyd, but still we all make a deal, magically witless as we are: we all come to terms. I switch off the bedside lamp, and leaving the window open, listen for the last of the fox cries.

It's almost comforting to hear them, year after year, their brief revelry shattering the stillness of the winter nights, their shrieking a language far older than our own. It occurs to me then, as I drift back to sleep, that they're not shrieking, those fugitive foxes, but laughing. Laughing and exulting in life, dancing their weird annual ritual on the lawns of the world, a carnival, for just a few nights, before dissolving into the shadows of the hedgerows and the dunes, slowly slipping away, gone again, leaving a trail of silence in the dew under the sapphire glow of Venus, the morning star.

Note: Translations from Huw Llwyd's Welsh from 'Medieval Welsh Lyrics' by Joseph Clancy.

A Letter about Resilience

From Kristian to Zoë

Iloved that poem by Samuel Green. It was awful to think about the damaged men, yet I couldn't stop reading for the next details, the next evidence, and that sweet, soft, simple ending, kneeling, healing, the silence, the clicking of the heels. The memory of grace within the memory of trauma. It's very deep.

Yes, I'm becoming increasingly open to the idea that men, working-class men, men like me, are harmed by patriarchy too. The body as commodity and instrument. If time is a quality of the imagination, which is to say, the soul, well then we are forced to sell far too much for almost nothing in return. Here in Bridgend, I encounter closed, violent, isolated men every day. Macho bullshit. Inherited damage now perhaps. All of which is to say maybe that class is as relevant as ever in Britain, as Brexit has reminded us.

But sometimes, mentioning class can seem as if we want to downplay the importance of race and gender in some way. Hopefully the opposite is true.

Yes, those pictures of protesters were shocking, but we seem to be consistently lowering the bar these days, new low after new low. People vote against their own interests, as we know. Facts don't change minds: imagination does, emotion does. Lies and fears dominate the headlines and control the narrative. The unconscious decides and then the mind later justifies and rationalises. It seems that what we need is a story, a powerful myth that gives our lives meaning and significance. We're not rational creatures. Far from it.

Many people seem to believe we will somehow get back to normal. But what was normal? Precarious work, low wages, austerity, disaster capitalism? A system recklessly overstretched to achieve maximum efficiency turns out to be completely vulnerable to shocks. It has no depth at all. There will be no going back.

Climate change, mass extinction and ecosystem collapse: get used to it. Ocean ecosystems are in such a ragged state that they could literally collapse tomorrow. The consequences of such an event are almost unimaginable but these things are now in play. We need deep local and state resilience and flexibility in order to be prepared for further and harder shocks or we will repeat this COVID-19 fiasco again and again. Maybe emergency is the new normal.

Into Eros

Zoë Brigley

c/w violence against women

I am here to tell you what I have been most ashamed of. The first man I fell in love with when I was only 15 raped me, not just once but many times. I loved a man who didn't love me back the way he was supposed to. No, he loved me by humiliating me, and I wonder now if it was all a test to see how far my love could stretch. But I am also here to say that I am determined to pass through and beyond it. I want you to know that I am not ashamed anymore.

In *Eros the Bittersweet*, Anne Carson talks about desire and love. "As Socrates tells it," she says, "your story begins the moment Eros enters you. That incursion is the biggest risk of your life." Yes, it is indeed a risk, but Carson doesn't talk about what happens when the gamble goes bad. How do we rebuild ourselves when we have given ourselves up to someone, trusted them, and been violated? Carson doesn't talk about fear.

I don't know if I would feel afraid if I saw him again. We haven't met for at least 15 years and there is so much I find hard to remember. But some things I recall like yesterday: moments of pain and humiliation. I have woken up with a shock at night remembering, or there have been times when in a normal day, I flash back, come over dizzy like I want to cry.

Somehow despite all that, Eros still strikes me, what Anne Carson translating Sappho calls the "limb loosener .../ sweet bitter, impossible to fight off, creature stealing up". It comes over me in cycles like changing seasons. I look for it in nature: in the lush, hot wind that passes over the flat Ohio land where I live. Some nights I doze sitting out on the patio, only a slight breeze moving among the trees, in my hair, across closed eyelids, my skin sensitive as a seismometer to the sensuousness of things.

I am so tired of answering the question: why did you stay with him for so long? Why does anyone stay with a person who abuses them? I could begin with me at 15 with body dysmorphia, how I doodled myself as a monster, loathed my physical appearance, and most of the time lapsed into silence. I was so thin that my teachers were worried that I had anorexia: no match for a boy, let alone a large man. I could begin with him at 20, a student studying geology; with the two of us meeting and how he told me that though I wasn't pretty or beautiful, I had a light that shone out of me that only he noticed. Already I was becoming dependent on him: the only person who would ever, could ever love someone like me, I thought at the time.

I have learned since not to regard myself, or to care about

my appearance, but to look out at the world, at the beauty out there. Like one morning, an Ohio squall passes through, and under the storm-light, the pumpkin flowers open up to the rain. The male flowers have been blooming for weeks, but the female flowers are new, and only open themselves up for a few hours in the morning. They are luminous yellow, incandescent. The petals are open, pressed back, and submissive somehow like a wild creature folding back its ears: the stigma in the middle of the flower like a nipple. The pumpkin flowers stand engorged without shame or fear.

It was a terrible shock: he had given himself up to my pleasure until we had penetrative sex - then everything changed. That first time, I thought he would stop when I told him how terrified I was. I know that I said no. After the first rape, I rang up a friend, told her how painful it had been, and she told me it was normal. I struggled to understand, went into denial. The second time he raped me was after he told me he was dumping me. We were walking home from the pub, and when he said the words, my legs collapsed under me. He carried me back to the house, proceeded to take off my clothes while I cried hysterically. What kind of a person sees a teenager beside herself with grief and decides they want to violently fuck her? Of course, he didn't actually break up with me.

Sometimes I still feel afraid, especially when I am in the

house alone at night or walking during the day. I have a regular walk through the woods by the railroad track. One day I am walking there by myself among the trees when a sound startles me: a creaking, like a door opening on its hinges, and I'm overcome with fear. Logically, I know it's just a creaking branch in the wind, but it seems too human, like a door opening, and someone might step through it, someone unwelcome. Is this what memory feels like after trauma?

For years, I puzzle over the why of what he did. Eventually, somehow, I manage to get his email, and we make smalltalk at first. He says he can imagine me walking a dog in the fall leaves. He tells me that he read my first book and calls me his "friend - nudge nudge wink wink". Then I send him a poem about the second time he raped me. He writes back saying he had no idea I was crying, that he wants to hold me and make sure I am ok. Do I want to meet for a drink? I write that another of his exes told me that the first time they had sex, she had no choice. He tells me he doesn't feel very nice. He says he is trying to remember what happened. I ask him, what do you think happened?

Is it possible for someone to be an abuser and not know what they are? Can you fuck someone who is crying or begging you not to, and still feel in the right? Is he gaslighting me, or trying to maintain plausible deniability? Is he afraid and guilty now? Does he wonder who I will tell?

What is the cost of all this violence? Some things that he did are unspeakable. Some things I have forgotten or want to forget. I could tell every humiliating thing that I remember, but who is to say that someone reading this wouldn't be turned on? Even now I feel shame: a sharp voice repeating: it's your fault, it's your fault, it's you, it's you.

But something was left behind that has kept me alive: the girl I was before the rapes - she's still here. A girl who daydreamed about Eros, was never ashamed of desire, but felt it running through her like electricity or blood. Recently I dreamed of a man who could change himself into a butterfly: a great black swallowtail. *You can do it too*, he told me, and before long, I could.

I have found my own pleasure before. I will again, but it's not easy to escape the fear. How to find the balance between the loving I need, and the risk and danger, the violence even of Eros: sweet bitter, limb loosener. But who can resist the gorgeousness of the world, the pull of the heart, the sensuous nature of things? Like the luminous pumpkin flowers opening and closing, opening and closing their narrow buds.

A Postscript about Optimism

From Kristian to Zoë

FEELINGS of aftermath, convalescence, the return to health. The 'dwellers' we are conjuring are not warriors then – conquering the world with 'necessary' violence — no, they are more likely to behave like, well... I'm picturing Charlie Chaplin! I loved those films as a kid. Chaplin's "Tramp" is tough and pugnacious to be sure, but he's also open-eyed with wonder, empathy, gentleness, generosity. He has a welcoming open-hearted optimistic determination to keep exploring, despite every setback, trying new things. Yes, his trust and generosity are a kind of hard-earned road-wisdom. He keeps trying. He always decides to choose life.

Acknowledgements

Writing from this chapbook was published in the UK - *Planet, Wales Arts Review,* and *Kenfig Journal* – and in the US: *The Nasiona* and *About Place.* Thanks to the editors of these journals and publications.

LAY OUT YOUR UNREST

Lightning Source UK Ltd.
Milton Keynes UK
UKHW011823080921
390221UK00002B/126